MW01139871

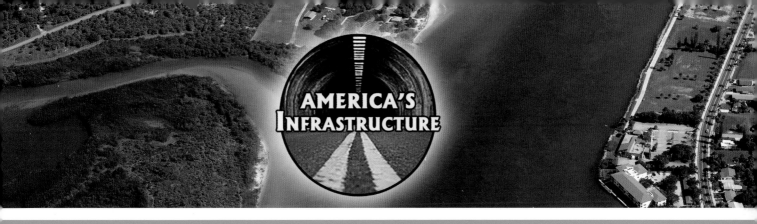

AMERICA'S INFRASTRUCTURE

Infrastructure of AMERICA'S Bridges

Marty Gitlin

Mitchell Lane
PUBLISHERS
2001 SW 31st Avenue
Hallandale, FL 33009
www.mitchelllane.com

Mitchell Lane
PUBLISHERS

Printing   1   2   3   4   5   6   7   8

Design: Sharon Beck
Editor: Jim Whiting

Library of Congress Cataloging-in-Publication Data
Names: Gitlin, Marty, author.
Title: Infrastructure of America's bridges / by Marty Gitlin.
Description: Hallandale, FL : Mitchell Lane Publishers, 2018. | Series: Engineering feats |
    Includes bibliographical references and index. | Audience: Ages 9-13.
Identifiers: LCCN 2017052252 | ISBN 9781680201406 (library bound)
Subjects: LCSH: Bridges—United States—Juvenile literature. | Bridges—United States—Safety
    measures—Juvenile literature.
Classification: LCC TG148 .G58 2018 | DDC 624.20973—dc23
LC record available at https://lccn.loc.gov/2017052252

eBook ISBN: 9-781-68020-141-3

ONTENTS

INTRODUCTION: Repairing Bridges 4

CHAPTER 1: Verrazano-Narrows Bridge 7

CHAPTER 2: Golden Gate Bridge 11

CHAPTER 3: Yankee Doodle Bridge 17

CHAPTER 4: Skagit River Bridge 21

CHAPTER 5: Arlington Memorial Bridge 25

CHAPTER 6: Storrow Drive Overpass 29

CHAPTER 7: Centennial Bridge 33

CHAPTER 8: Greensboro Bridge 37

WHAT YOU SHOULD KNOW 40

TIMELINE 41

CHAPTER NOTES 42

FURTHER READING 44

ON THE INTERNET 44

WORKS CONSULTED 44

GLOSSARY 46

INDEX 47

ABOUT THE AUTHOR 48

Words in **bold** throughout can be found in the Glossary.

Repairing Bridges

The date was December 15, 1967. The time was 5:00 p.m. People who had just left work were driving home on the Silver Bridge that spanned the Ohio River between West Virginia and Ohio.

Suddenly, a loud noise that sounded like a gunshot rang out. The bridge began to collapse. Thirty-two cars dropped into the freezing water. Forty-six people who seconds earlier had been looking forward to a relaxing evening at home were now plunging to their deaths.

A study revealed that a broken metal bar along the bridge had caused the disaster. The flaw had developed from **corrosion** (kuh-ROH-zhuhn) over 40 years since the bridge was built.

A task force began examining bridges throughout the United States. It evaluated **standards** (STAN-derds) used to ensure their safety and provided ideas to guard against another disaster.[1]

But America has been tempting fate ever since. Many of its bridges remain in terrible shape. A 2016 study claimed that more than 58,000 of them needed repairs. Millions of drivers cross those bridges every day. The threat of more deadly accidents seems very real.[2]

Government officials have promised to spend more on **infrastructure** (IN-fruh-struk-shur) projects such as bridge repair. But they rarely agree on

Q & A

What bridge collapsed in a windstorm just four months after it opened?
The Narrows Bridge in Tacoma, Washington opened in July 1940 and collapsed that November. Fortunately no one was killed.

Powerful winds wreaked havoc with the original Tacoma Narrows Bridge on the day of its collapse in 1940.

how much to **earmark** (EER-mark) for such plans. They also argue about how those funds should be spent.

Some of the busiest bridges are in the worst shape. They require repairs that will take years to complete. Billions of dollars will be needed to fix them. But the effort will be worth every penny if it saves lives.

Bridges provide a valuable service to millions of Americans. Drivers of cars, trucks, and buses need sturdy spans to pass over lakes, rivers, valleys, railroad tracks, and even parts of oceans. Those behind the wheel require peace of mind. Reports of bridge collapses make them feel unsafe. They need to know which bridges are strong and which are not.

When were they built? How did they get into such poor condition? What repairs do they need? What will it cost to make them safe?

Every troubled bridge has its own unique history. The following chapters provide details about eight of the most interesting ones.

The Verrazano-Narrows Bridge hovers above the guided-missile cruiser USS *Leyte Gulf*. The bridge connects the New York boroughs of Brooklyn and Staten Island. The inset shows a statue of Giovanni da Verrazzano, for whom the bridge was named. The statue is located in Battery Park in New York City.

CHAPTER 1
Verrazano-Narrows Bridge

Giovanni da Verrazzano (vair-uh-ZAH-no) was the first European to explore the area now known as New York City. He and his crew sailed there in 1524. They traveled the land and became friends with the local Indians. His memory was honored when the Verrazano-Narrows Bridge opened in 1964.

The span connects the **boroughs** (BUHR-ohs) of Brooklyn and Staten Island. It is the longest **suspension bridge** (suh-SPEN-shuhn BRIJ) in the United States at 4,260 feet and the 11th-longest in the world. It stands above the Narrows, a mile-long waterway that enters New York Harbor.

Construction began in 1959. Hundreds of homes were destroyed to make room. Workers called "punks" lugged heavy bolts. They delivered them to foremen called "pushers." The bridge opened in 1964. Building it cost $320 million, which translates to $2.5 billion today.

The project also changed Staten Island. The people there had lived as if in a village, far away from the hustle and bustle of New York. They enjoyed the almost rural feel of their community. They could only reach the city by ferry boat. But now the bridge allowed them to cross by car. They became tied forever to New York City.

Q & A
How many workers did it take to construct the Verrazano-Narrows Bridge?
About 10,000 men were used to build the structure.

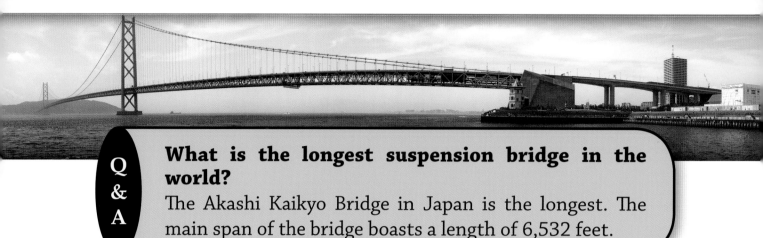

What is the longest suspension bridge in the world?
The Akashi Kaikyo Bridge in Japan is the longest. The main span of the bridge boasts a length of 6,532 feet.

Drivers at first paid 50 cents to use the bridge, the equivalent of $4 today. But today they must shell out $15 for the same trip. The cost does not prevent about 1.5 million drivers from crossing the bridge every week. It allows them to get to and from Staten Island much faster.[1]

It is natural that a 50-year-old span would need work to remain safe. Construction plans were announced in 2016. Some drivers were upset to learn that it would take about 25 years to complete.

"This is daunting and disheartening, if not depressing," said Staten Island Borough President James Oddo. "It's going to be a difficult thing for Staten Islanders to accept but the reality is that this work needs to happen."[2]

Nobody knows why the name of Giovanni da Verrazzano is misspelled in the name of the Verrazano-Narrows Bridge. One "z" is missing. That upset Brooklyn college student Robert Nash. He began a campaign to correct the name of the bridge. The New York State Senate passed a bill in 2017 to try to achieve that goal. But some people have complained that adding the letter to all the signs could cost millions of dollars.[3]

The proposal called for $1.5 billion to fix the bridge. Work on the upper deck and Staten Island Expressway soon began. It also started quickly on the Belt Parkway ramps to the island. The plan included studies that would lead to the construction of bike and **pedestrian** (puh-DES-tree-uhn) paths.

Planners believe the upper deck replacement will make the bridge stronger. Lighter steel that lasts longer was installed after the original roadway was destroyed. A new lane was added. Old decking was removed and replaced by 938 new panels. New cement and waterproofing were added to strengthen the bridge.[4]

Road work makes it harder for drivers on the Verrazano-Narrows Bridge. Lanes closed on both the upper and lower levels as workers toiled to complete the job. But many drivers were happy despite having fewer lanes to choose from. They knew they were driving on a bridge that would soon be stronger and safer.

Crews shown here in May 2015 are busily working to repair the upper level of the Verrazano-Narrows Bridge.

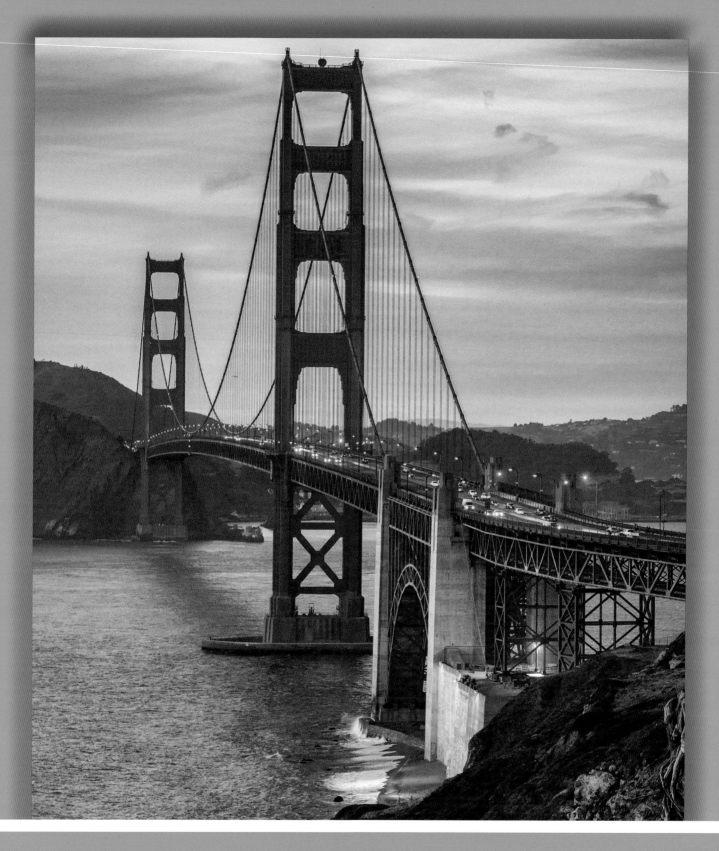

The majestic Golden Gate Bridge, seen here lit up in the summer twilight hours, can look as beautiful as its surroundings. The mountains near the city of San Francisco are visible in the background.

CHAPTER 2
Golden Gate Bridge

The Golden Gate Bridge is perhaps the most famous bridge in the United States. It is certainly among the most beautiful. Its name has nothing to do with the color. The bridge was named after the Golden Gate Strait, the entrance to San Francisco from the Pacific Ocean. The color is actually a distinct reddish orange. Its two grand towers soar 746 feet into the sky. Cars zoom high above the sparkling waters of the San Francisco Bay.

Life was not beautiful for most Americans when construction began in 1933. It was the low point of the Great Depression. Millions of people had lost their jobs. But many found work through building projects. Nobody knows how many workers toiled to erect the Golden Gate Bridge.[1] What is known is that 11 were killed in the process, though that is fewer than what had been expected for such a massive job. Ten of them lost their lives in one accident on February 17, 1937. A platform carrying them hundreds of feet in the air gave way and fell through the safety net. That net saved 19 others during the project.[2]

The efforts of all the workers would be greatly admired. They did not just get the job done in four years. They also kept costs down. The project

Q & A

How much did the workers who built the bridge earn for their efforts?

They were paid $11 per day.

This 1935 photo shows the Golden Gate Bridge during its construction phase.

finished under budget at $35 million. That translates to more than $1 billion today.

The importance of such a bridge had been evident for years. The only way people could get across the bay had been by ferry boat. The design for the Golden Gate Bridge was created by **architect** (AHR-ki-tekt) Irving Morrow. He rejected the typical black and gray color for reddish orange. Morrow had logical reasons for his choice. He figured it would be easier to

The Golden Gate Bridge as it is being built.

spot by those on passing ships. The United States Navy liked the idea. Its officials even wanted black and yellow stripes added to make it even easier to see.[3]

Among the unique features of the bridge are its fog horns. On the bay's frequently foggy days, the horns can be heard clear across the city. Each horn boasts a different pitch. They tell those navigating the ships whether to stay to the right or to the left of the bridge towers.[4] Workers keep the bridge bright with frequent painting. That protects it from the

ocean salt water in the air that rusts the steel. The suspension on the Golden Gate Bridge spans 4,200 feet. It was the longest span in the world until the Verrazano-Narrows Bridge in New York City opened in 1964. Since then many other longer ones have been built around the world.

More than two billion vehicles have crossed the Golden Gate Bridge since it opened in 1937. But the paint jobs that prevent rust have not stopped age from taking a toll. Wear and tear appear throughout the cables holding up the bridge.

Complaints about the main cable extend back to 1969. It was recommended then that it be painted immediately. **Engineers** (in-juh-NEERZ) claimed that the main cable should be replaced. But neither job was ever done. One official stated that the bracing on the underside of the bridge was all rusty.

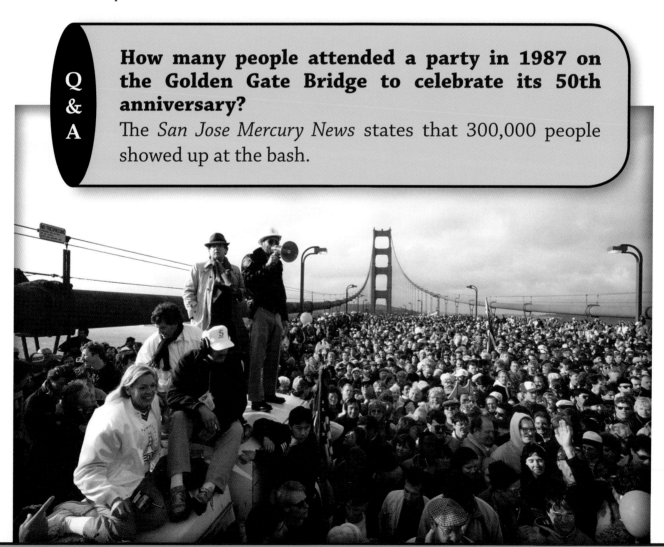

Q & A

How many people attended a party in 1987 on the Golden Gate Bridge to celebrate its 50th anniversary?

The *San Jose Mercury News* states that 300,000 people showed up at the bash.

A devastating earthquake on October 17, 1989 led to the heaviest traffic ever on the Golden Gate Bridge. The quake damaged the Bay Bridge between San Francisco and Oakland. Commuters were diverted to the unharmed Golden Gate Bridge. The result was that it provided passage for 162,414 vehicles on October 27. That remains a one-day record.[5]

Millions of dollars were set aside in 2011 to pay for a painting of the rusting cables. But it was spent instead on other projects. It was later hoped that more funds would result in the job being completed by 2022.[6]

The Golden Gate Bridge brings pride to the people of San Francisco and the entire nation. Keeping it safe would help keep that pride alive.

The Yankee Doodle Bridge is among 357 bridges in the state of Connecticut that have been deemed "structurally deficient." It is shown here carrying significant car and truck traffic.

CHAPTER 3
Yankee Doodle Bridge

The song "Yankee Doodle" is among the oldest and most famous tunes related to American history. Its lyrics feature three words: Yankee Doodle Dandy. But there is nothing dandy about the Yankee Doodle Bridge. The span over the Norwalk River in Connecticut was given a "poor" rating by the U.S. Department of Transportation in 2016.[1]

The name of the bridge is connected to the song. Legend claims that the man nicknamed Yankee Doodle lived in Norwalk. The lyrics state that he rode on a pony with a feather in his hat.

Research provides some evidence that Yankee Doodle was a real person. His name was Thomas Fitch. Fitch was the son of a Connecticut governor. He led a group of Norwalk men to fight alongside the British during the French and Indian War of the 1750s. As Fitch and his men were leaving Norwalk, his sister Elizabeth placed chicken feathers in their caps. When they arrived at their destination, a British Army doctor named Richard Shuckburgh was inspired to write the familiar "Yankee Doodle" tune.[2]

Q & A

The lyrics of "Yankee Doodle" include "stuck a feather in his hat and called it macaroni." What does that mean?
Song Facts claims that "macaroni" was a term at that time for a well-dressed man. The line implies that American men thought they could look good simply by sticking a feather in their hats.

The song became so famous that its title was used to name the Norwalk bridge when it was built in 1957. It has become one of the busiest bridges in Connecticut. An average of 146,000 vehicles cross it daily. There is plenty of room, as the bridge features four lanes in each direction.

Its poor grade does not mean it is in danger of collapse. Every bridge is inspected at least once every two years in Connecticut. Those in worse shape are examined more often. Officials there have stated that they would close any bridge believed to

The Yankee Doodle Bridge is in bad shape. But in general, Connecticut bridges are in much better shape than those in other states. Less than one in 10 bridges in that state are in bad condition. At the other extreme, more than one in five bridges in Rhode Island, Pennsylvania, and Iowa are ranked poor or worse.

Q & A

How wide is the Yankee Doodle Bridge?
Its overall width is just under 122 feet. The roadway itself is 108 feet wide.

be unsafe. Connecticut had already suffered through such a disaster. A bridge over the Manus River in Greenwich collapsed in 1983. Three drivers were killed.

The Yankee Doodle Bridge was simply deemed in need of repair. The plan was to fix it before it became dangerous. A total of $25 million was earmarked for the project. But the work was put off until 2018. That is when it would be combined with work to resurface an attached highway in the Norwalk area. The cost of the two projects combined is $50 million. The date of completion is set for late 2020.

Two new guard rails will be installed. So will **median** (MEE-dee-uhn) dividers and a new fender system around the bridge piers in the river.

This underneath look at the Yankee Doodle Bridge shows some of its corrosion.

Included will also be painting and repairs to the underside of the deck. The steel and deck expansion joints will be improved as well.

The entire work area for the two projects will stretch more than two miles from the Saugatuck River Bridge to the Yankee Doodle Bridge.[3]

Debate has raged in Norwalk about whether Yankee Doodle really existed. But there is no argument that the Yankee Doodle Bridge needs to remain safe. The work set to start in 2018 should ensure that it will. And that will make the Yankee Doodle dandy again.

The collapse of the Skagit River Bridge on the route between the cities of Seattle and Vancouver, Canada was caused by a truck hitting one of its trusses. The inset shows the bridge before the 2013 accident.

CHAPTER 4
Skagit River Bridge

Truck driver William Scott was approaching the Skagit River Bridge in Mt. Vernon, Washington in the early evening of May 23, 2013. The bridge is an important part of the link between the big cities of Seattle and Vancouver, Canada on Interstate 5. An average of 71,000 vehicles cross it daily.

Scott believed the height of his oversized truck was two inches shorter than it really was. The top of his truck clipped a beam. It created just a small crack, but a huge disaster. An entire section of the bridge fell into the Skagit River. Scott made it across the span. Two vehicles behind him carrying three people dropped into the water.[1]

They were lucky. They were rescued and suffered only minor injuries. But police officer Sean O'Connell was killed later. He was directing traffic along a detour following the bridge collapse when his motorcycle collided with a truck.

Scott was at fault for not knowing the height of his truck. But the accident could probably have been avoided had the bridge been stronger and in better shape.

The bridge was built in 1955. It was 58 years old at the time. But the problem was not due to corrosion or age. It was the result of weak construction. A study of the collapse blamed its original design. That

 Q & A **What is the length of the Skagit River Bridge?**
It is 1,120 feet long.

Vance Creek Bridge in a remote Washington State forest is the second-highest railway trestle in the U.S. For years after being abandoned by the railroads, a few hardy hikers visited it every year. Then in 2012 it became a social media sensation. Many people trooped there. Some vandalized it and scrawled graffiti. The company that owns the bridge closed it.

allowed a tiny crack in one part to lead to a chain reaction of more failures.

Engineers Tim Stark and Jim LaFave helped research the disaster. LaFave suggested design changes to strengthen similar bridges. After all, the beam hit by Scott's truck was not a major component. LaFave also suggested added support beams to handle impact. That way the bridge could remain stable and standing.

The collapse caused major headaches for many people. The repairs totaled $15 million. And that does not include lost money for businesses in the area. Many potential customers stayed away because they no longer

Q & A

How were the drivers of the three vehicles that fell into the Skagit River rescued?
Rescuers included the U.S. Coast Guard. The Whidbey Island Naval Air Station sent a helicopter. The county sheriff dispatched a boat. The rescue was also assisted by the Mount Vernon and Burlington police and fire departments.

had access to the highway by crossing the bridge. It was a financial disaster as well as a structural one.

Engineers such as Stark and LaFave warned of other potential bridge disasters around the country. They stated that those with similar designs could also collapse for the same reasons. There are more than 10,000 such bridges throughout the United States.[2]

Maybe more vehicles will be on those bridges the next time a minor beam is clipped. Perhaps their drivers will be less lucky than those passing over the Skagit River on that fateful May evening. They were saved. Others might not be. There is always the threat of human error. The bridges of the future must be built to withstand impact. That is a lesson to be learned.

Four immense statues grace the Arlington Memorial Bridge in Washington, D.C. The insets depict Valor (left) and Sacrifice (right), located at the east end of the bridge.

CHAPTER 5
Arlington Memorial Bridge

Many people believe the Arlington Memorial Bridge is the most beautiful bridge in Washington, D.C., the capital of the United States. It spans the Potomac (puh-TOH-muhk) River from the Lincoln Memorial to the Arlington House in Virginia. The Arlington House was once the home of Confederate General Robert E. Lee.

Nine broad arches carry the bridge 2,163 feet across the river. Except for the draw span, it is made of reinforced concrete.

An unusual and elegant feature of the bridge is the four bronze statues of heroes on horseback. Two, "The Art of War," are located on the eastern end of the bridge. "Valor" displays a male rider and a female striding forward with a shield. "Sacrifice" highlights a female representing the earth looking up to the rider Mars.

The two statues on the other side are "The Art of Peace." "Music and Harvest" consists of a winged horse between a man carrying a bundle of wheat and a woman with a harp. "Aspiration and Literature" features another winged horse flanked by figures holding a book and a bow. The statues were commissioned in 1925, seven years before the bridge was constructed. But they were not erected until 1951.[1]

 **Q & A** **How tall are the four statues that grace the Arlington Memorial Bridge?**
They are 17 feet tall.

If the statues could talk, they would say the bridge needs repairs. It turned 85 years old in 2017. It badly needs a makeover. It became such a mess that the National Park Service was forced to make emergency repairs while a major **restoration** (reh-stuh-RAY-shuhn) remained in the planning stages. The goal of the restoration plan is to improve or replace the original bridge parts while maintaining its character and beauty.

Among the specific elements will be repairing the concrete arches and stone fronts of the 10 spans. The steel structure of the span will be replaced. The bridge deck and sidewalks are also scheduled for new construction. The travel lanes will be resurfaced.

Washington, D.C. mayor Muriel Bowser made a plea to the U.S. government in January 2017. She asked for money to pay for Arlington Memorial Bridge repairs. A grant for $90 million had been approved in 2016. But $160 million more would be needed to get the job done.[2]

The Arlington Memorial Bridge has nine arches. The center arch is the bascule, which is movable to allow boats to pass through.

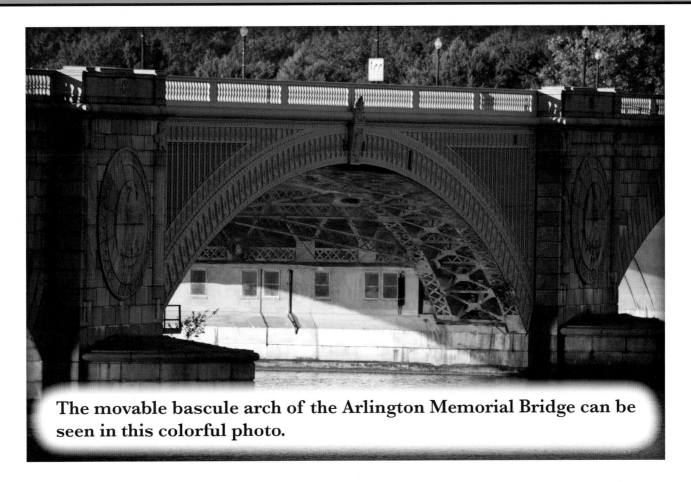

The movable bascule arch of the Arlington Memorial Bridge can be seen in this colorful photo.

The overhaul was deemed necessary by the Federal Highway Administration. Its officials claimed that the bridge would eventually become too dangerous to remain open and said they would have to close it by 2021 without major repairs. The FHA was especially concerned about the concrete deck. No vehicle weighing more than 10 tons will be allowed to cross the bridge until it has been fixed.

The project is expected to cost at least $250 million. It will be one of the most expensive repairs in National Park Service history. But the Arlington Memorial Bridge carries an average of 68,000 vehicles a day. Ensuring their safety makes it worth every penny.[3]

Q & A

How wide are the sidewalks for pedestrian traffic along the bridge?
The sidewalks are 15 feet wide.

The heavy traffic on Storrow Drive in Boston can be seen in this view from the pedestrian overpass. Cars are shown here heading into the tunnel.

CHAPTER 6
Storrow Drive Overpass

Storrow Drive Overpass is part of a double-deck roadway bordering the Back Bay area in Boston, Massachusetts. An average of about 60,000 cars head west on it every day.

It takes most bridges decades to weaken. The problem is most acute in the Northeast. Salt poured over roads to melt ice in the winter results in corrosion. Years of heavy traffic and bad weather also take a toll on a bridge.

A slow decline was not the case with the Storrow Drive Tunnel. Problems were detected soon after it opened in 1951. They have gotten worse. In 2013, *Travel + Leisure* magazine ranked it the most dangerous bridge in the United States.[1] The magazine analyzed information from the Federal Highway Administration and focused on bridges handling daily traffic of at least 50,000 vehicles. It stated that the pavement of the upper deck is too thick. That has led to corrosion on steel beams that support it.

Many Boston drivers were shocked to learn that their bridge was rated the most dangerous. They were further stunned to learn that it received a **sufficiency** (suh-FISH-uhn-see) rating of zero.[2]

Massachusetts state officials refuted the report. They claimed that the bridge and tunnel were safe for travel. They argued that repairs had indeed

Q & A

How much would it cost to replace the Storrow Drive Tunnel?

The price tag is estimated to be about $200 million.

been made. But they served only to keep traffic flowing through 2018. That is when long-term solutions are expected to be explored.[3] Experts in the state have complained that not enough money has been provided to spend on a permanent fix.[4]

One idea is placing a tax on gas purchases to help pay for repairs. The millions of dollars needed to fix the bridge completely must come from somewhere.[5] President Donald Trump promised that money would be spent to strengthen infrastructure throughout the country. But nobody knew if or when that would happen. Or if it could be done in time to fix the Storrow Road Tunnel before it became too dangerous.

The road has been the center of debate since the late 1940s. It was decided to build Storrow Drive through a beloved park called the Esplanade. The park lies along the Back Bay with the Charles River running through it.

Q & A **How did the Charles River in Boston get its name?**
Seventeen-century English explorer John Smith gave it that name to honor King Charles I.

Trees hover over this footbridge, which heads toward the famous Charles River of Boston.

Demolition of the Longfellow Bridge over Storrow Drive heading west in Boston is seen here.

Many people who loved the park protested. They became angrier when the road was named after James Storrow. He was a Boston banker and lawyer who worked to preserve and improve the park. They believed that naming the road was an insult to him. Storrow has been dead for nearly 100 years. Many believe he would be rolling over in his grave had he known that a road named after him was built through the park. Or that the bridge in his beloved hometown of Boston was deemed the most dangerous in America.[6]

James and Helen Storrow were known for their work in scouting. Helen was an international Girl Scout leader. James was the president of the Boy Scouts of America from 1925 until he died in 1926. The two met while scaling the Matterhorn mountain in Switzerland.[7]

The curving Centennial Bridge is the site of this St. Patrick's Day parade. The event took its participants from Illinois into Iowa.

CHAPTER 7
Centennial Bridge

Many states have more bridges than Iowa. But no state is saddled with a larger number of bad bridges. A 2017 study claimed that nearly 5,000 Iowa spans were in poor condition. That is more than one in five bridges statewide.[1]

The Centennial Bridge is the most traveled among them. Its five-span steel arch runs 4,447 feet and its suspended deck hovers 66 feet above the Mississippi River to connect Rock Island, Illinois, and Davenport, Iowa.[2] About 32,000 vehicles cross daily.

The Centennial Bridge opened in 1940, making it 78 years old in 2018. It remains in sorry shape despite extensive repairs in 2014 and 2015.

John Wegmeyer of the Illinois Department of Transportation gave an unusual reason for its low rating. He blamed a lack of space on which drivers can pull off. He also admitted that the arched span must be replaced. But that will cost millions of dollars. "It's been something talked about for years," he said. "We know we need to replace the bridge. There's only so much money available."[3]

Minor Centennial Bridge deck repairs in 2015 cost more than $3 million. It was shut down in 2014 while two beams spanning its 46-foot width

Q & A

What are the populations of Rock Island, Illinois, and Davenport, Iowa?

The 2016 census shows that the population of Rock Island is 38,210 and the population of Davenport is 102,612.

were replaced. The bridge was set to reopen that September. But work on the handrail and concrete median kept it closed. "There are a thousand members of that bridge getting old," Wegmeyer added. "All the joints, everything riveted and bolted together. . . . We're making repairs . . . to keep it safe. . . . The only way to get much better is to replace it."[4]

The five arches of the Centennial Bridge are shown here. The two largest symbolize the towns of Rock Island, Illinois, and Davenport, Iowa.

The bridge would never have existed if not for the persistence of Rock Island mayor Robert Galbraith. He visited the state capital and nation's capital more than 60 times in the late 1930s to gain permission to build it. He received no government funds. Driver tolls paid for the project.

Construction began in March 1939. The bridge opened in early June 1940. A dedication ceremony followed five weeks later. About 57,000

Q & A

How much steel was used to build the Centennial Bridge?

Nearly 10,000 tons of steel were used.

vehicles and 20,000 pedestrians crossed in the first eight hours after the event.

The engineers who built the bridge bragged about the simple design. They boasted that it was the only four-lane bridge across the Mississippi River with two lanes in both directions. They crowed about charging less than any toll bridge on the Mississippi and that it cost the taxpayers nothing.[5] Galbraith proved unselfish in the naming of the bridge. It was to be named after him. But he suggested calling it the Rock Island Centennial Bridge. That name honored the 100th anniversary of the city's founding.

Car drivers originally paid 10 cents to use the bridge. Pedestrians were charged five cents. The toll for cars reached 50 cents in 1991. Truck drivers paid more than two dollars.

Research showed that too many vehicles were using other area bridges, mostly due to the tolls. An agreement allowed Illinois and Iowa to share ownership in 2005. They removed the toll booths. Traffic picked up after that. It grew from an average of 16,000 to 31,000 per day by the end of 2005.[6]

The tolls are gone. But age has certainly taken a toll on the Centennial Bridge. It is no wonder that state officials admit it must be replaced.

The Rock Island company Dohrn Transfer owned the first vehicle to pay a toll to cross the Centennial Bridge. Amazingly, the same company also owned the last vehicle that had to pay a toll to cross the bridge about 60 years later.[7]

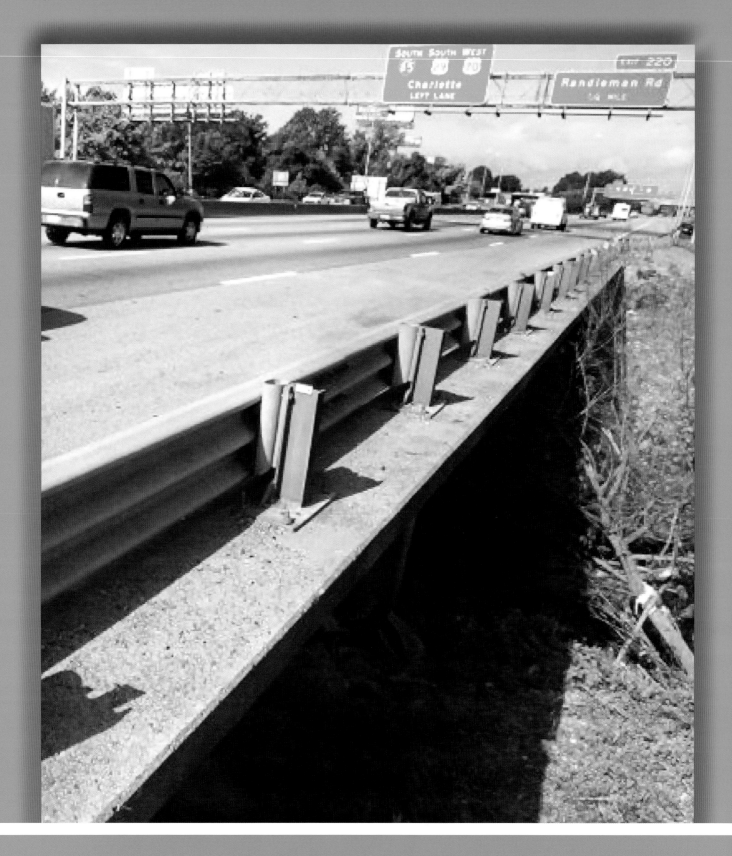

A glimpse of the underside of the Greensboro Bridge can be seen here as traffic crosses it. The bridge spans South Buffalo Creek in the North Carolina city that bears its name.

Chapter 8
Greensboro Bridge

At least the Greensboro Bridge is dependable. It can be counted on to be rated the worst bridge in North Carolina. It ranked dead last in five of the past six years through 2017.

The span hovers over South Buffalo Creek at the intersection of Interstates 40 and 85 in Guilford County.

The bridge is 62 years old and is falling apart. Chunks of concrete are visible at its base. How much of that problem is due to heavy traffic remains uncertain. An average of 123,000 vehicles cross it every day. That adds up to almost one million per week.[1]

Repairs are slated for 2019. Until then, drivers must believe promises by local officials that it is safe. Or they can find another path to their destinations.

The Department of Transportation puts only some stock in traffic volume. It uses engineers to analyze bridge conditions every two years. Its information plays the biggest role in determining which bridges are most badly in need of repair.

The DOT data is then used by the area American Automobile Association (AAA Carolinas). Triple-A provides people with its own ratings and rankings.

 When was the Greensboro Bridge built?
It was constructed in 1955.

Not enough evidence was found to motivate officials to close the Greensboro Bridge. But it has been obvious for years that work must be done. "If the **inspection** (in-SPEK-shuhn) reveals something has changed, the bridge would be closed immediately," said DOT spokeswoman Amanda Perry. "We're not going to put the public in danger."[2]

The amount of disrepair created by heavy traffic has been the subject of debate. State highway officials claim that Triple-A overrates that information. They believe that other bridges in North Carolina are in worse shape. Their argument is that those spans were not rated as badly by Triple-A because they do not receive as much traffic.

The Department of Transportation states that too much emphasis on traffic volume weakens the Triple-A rankings. The DOT considers volume of traffic. But it focuses more on the strength of the bridge and how long experts believe it can remain safe.

Department engineer Mike Mills prefers that outlook to the one used by Triple-A. He considers it more scientific. "Ours is more of an engineering decision than theirs," Mills said.

South Buffalo Creek is a headwater stream in the Cape Fear Basin. A movie titled *Cape Fear* might send chills down the spines of movie fans. It is about a madman who seeks revenge against a lawyer and his family. The climax of the film is a battle between the villain and hero on a scary boat ride at Cape Fear.

Q & A

How many of the 20 bridges ranked worst in North Carolina are in Guilford County?

There are 100 counties in North Carolina. But the Department of Transportation reports that Guilford County is the home of nine of the state's 20 worst bridges.

The Greensboro Bridge owns the dubious distinction of a top ranking on the Triple-A Substandard Bridge list in North Carolina.

The state has responded to previous reports. It spent nearly $500 million repairing and replacing bridges across the state in 2013 alone. That work greatly increased the number of North Carolina bridges deemed to be in good condition.[3]

Drivers in North Carolina do not care how information about faulty bridges is obtained. They do not care who provides it. They simply want to know which bridges are safe.

Experts in the state all seem to agree that Greensboro Bridge over South Buffalo Creek will be safe until repairs are completed in 2019. Those passing through can only hope they are right.

What You Should Know

◆ There are 614,387 bridges in the United States. A total of 56,007 were rated in poor condition in 2016.

◆ An estimated $123 billion would be needed to repair the bad bridges throughout the country.

◆ About four in 10 American bridges are 50 years of age or older.

◆ Drivers take an average of 188 million trips across structurally deficient bridges every day.

◆ Bridges have been built using several different materials, including wood, steel, iron, and concrete.

◆ There are six types of bridges: cable-stayed, truss, beam, arch, suspension, and cantilever.

◆ The first steel bridge in the United States opened in 1874. It spanned the Mississippi River near St. Louis, Missouri.

◆ The West Liberty Covered Bridge in Geneva, Ohio, is the shortest in the country. It is just 18 feet long. Some vehicles that cross are longer than the bridge itself.

◆ The highest bridge in the United States is the Royal Gorge Bridge, 1,053 feet above the ground. It is located in the Rocky Mountains in Colorado. It was the highest in the world until China's Beipanjiang River Bridge opened in 2003.

◆ The first large-span bridge in America was built over the Charles River in Cambridge, Massachusetts in 1622. It was constructed with heavy timber.

◆ Pennsylvania is the state with the highest number of covered bridges in America. It boasts 213. Ohio is second with 148.

◆ Repairs on the Brooklyn Bridge in New York began in 2010. They were scheduled to cost about $500 million and be done in 2017. But the cost rose to more than $800 million. And the timetable for completion was pushed back to 2022.

◆ The George Washington Bridge that connects the New York borough of Manhattan with New Jersey is the most-traveled bridge in America. More than 50 million vehicles pass eastbound every year. Its two decks total 14 lanes to accommodate the traffic.

◆ The Golden Gate Bridge in San Francisco is believed to be the most photographed bridge in the world. Its unique reddish orange color makes it attractive to photographers.

◆ The three longest bridges in the United States are all in Louisiana. They are the Lake Pontchartrain Causeway, Manchac Swamp Bridge, and Atchafayala Basin Bridge.

◆ The oldest covered bridge in America is the Permanent Bridge in Philadelphia, Pennsylvania. The 550-foot structure was built over the Schuylkill River in 1805.

◆ One New York bridge found its way into a famous song title. "The 59th Street Bridge Song" was a hit by the legendary Simon & Garfunkel in the 1960s. The song is also known as "Feelin' Groovy."

◆ One bridge connects two separate parts of a state. The Mackinac Bridge joins the lower and upper peninsulas of Michigan. It opened in 1957.

◆ The skirmish at North Bridge in Concord, Massachusetts was one of the first battles of the Revolutionary War.

TIMELINE

1697 The Frankford Avenue Bridge in northeast Pennsylvania opens and remains the oldest surviving bridge in the United States.

1883 The Brooklyn Bridge opens in New York City.

1929 The Royal Gorge suspension bridge in Colorado opens.

1931 Construction begins on the Storrow Drive Tunnel. The George Washington Bridge in New Jersey opens.

1932 The Arlington Memorial Bridge opens.

1933 Construction starts on the Golden Gate Bridge.

1936 The San Francisco-Oakland Bay Bridge opens.

1937 The Golden Gate Bridge opens.

1940 The Centennial Bridge in Davenport, Iowa opens.

1951 Storrow Drive Tunnel in Boston officially opens.

1956 The Lake Pontchartrain Causeway opens in southern Louisiana and remains the longest bridge in America at nearly 24 miles.

1957 The Mackinac suspension bridge linking the upper and lower peninsulas of Michigan opens.

1959 Construction begins on the Verrazano-Narrows Bridge.

1964 The Verrazano-Narrows Bridge opens.

1967 The Silver Bridge spanning West Virginia and Ohio collapses and 46 people are killed.

1980 Collapse of the Sunshine Skyway Bridge in Tampa, Florida, kills 35.

1993 A barge slams into on the Big Bayou Canot bridge in Mobile, Alabama, and causes a train derailment which kills 47 people.

2011 The 18-foot-long West Liberty Covered Bridge in Geneva, Ohio, opens as the shortest bridge in the United States.

2013 Part of the Skagit River Bridge in Mount Vernon, Washington collapses.

2017 The New York State Senate passes a bill to correct the spelling of the Verrazano-Narrows Bridge.

INTRODUCTION: Repairing Bridges

1. "Silver Bridge," West Virginia Department of Transportation. http://www.transportation.wv.gov/highways/bridge_facts/Modern-Bridges/Pages/Silver.aspx
2. Bart Jansen, "Study: 58,000 U.S. bridges found to be 'structurally deficient.'" *USA Today*. February 18, 2016. https://www.usatoday.com/story/news/2016/02/18/fewer-bridges-need-repairs-but-task-still-monumental/80512038/

Chapter 1: Verrazano-Narrows Bridge

1. Jerry Adler, "The history of the Verrazano-Narrows Bridge, 50 years after its construction." *Smithsonian*. November 2014. http://www.smithsonianmag.com/history/history-verrazano-narrows-bridge-50-years-after-its-construction-180953032/
2. Vincent Barone, "Decades of construction being planned for Verrazano-Narrows Bridge." SILive.com. October 15, 2015. http://www.silive.com/news/2015/10/decades_of_necessary_construct.html
3. "Did you know the Verrazano Bridge is spelled wrong?" *New York Post*. June 8, 2016. http://nypost.com/2016/06/08/did-you-know-the-verrazano-bridge-is-spelled-wrong/
4. Judy L. Randall, "A pothole-proof Verrazano? That's what engineers are promising." SILive. June 6, 2014. http://www.silive.com/news/index.ssf/2014/06/a_pothole-proof_verrazano_that.html

Chapter 2: Golden Gate Bridge

1. "Frequently asked questions about the Golden Gate Bridge." Goldengatebridge.org. http://goldengatebridge.org/research/facts.php#SFChron
2. Amy Standen, "75 years ago, a deadly day on the Golden Gate." NPR. May 27, 2012. http://www.npr.org/2012/05/27/153778083/75-years-later-building-the-golden-gate-bridge
3. "Frequently asked questions."
4. Annie Tittiger, "Golden Gate Bridge facts and trivia." TripSavvy.com. August 3, 2016. https://www.tripsavvy.com/golden-gate-bridge-facts-and-trivia-2939802
5. "Frequently asked questions."
6. Jeffrey Schaub, "The Golden Gate Bridge is starting to show its age." CBS Local. November 22, 2016. http://sanfrancisco.cbslocal.com/2016/11/22/the-golden-gate-bridge-is-starting-to-show-its-age/

Chapter 3: Yankee Doodle Bridge

1. Ana Radelat, "Report: Yankee Doodle Bridge in Norwalk 'structurally deficient.'" *Connecticut Mirror*. February 19, 2016. http://www.thehour.com/norwalk/article/Report-Yankee-Doodle-Bridge-in-Norwalk-8013016.php
2. Jeffrey Schmalz, "Was Yankee Doodle fact or fiction? Debate rages on in Norwalk." *New York Times*. April 19, 1984. http://www.nytimes.com/1984/04/19/nyregion/was-yankee-doodle-fact-of-fiction-fight-rages-on-in-norwalk.html
3. Frank Juliano, "Yankee Doodle Bridge work delayed until 2018." *Connecticut Post*. April 29, 2016. http://www.ctpost.com/local/article/Rehab-of-Yankee-Doodle-Bridge-over-I-95-pushed-7383820.php

Chapter 4: Skagit River Bridge

1. Mike Lindblom, "Skagit bridge documents: Did pilot-car poll strike crossbeams?" *Seattle Times*. June 11, 2014. http://blogs.seattletimes.com/today/2014/06/skagit-bridge-collapse-passing-trucker-thought-noise-was-a-bouncy-load/
2. Jennifer Ouellette, "New analysis confirms why the Skagit River Bridge collapsed." Gizmodo. August 27, 2016. http://gizmodo.com/new-analysis-confirms-why-the-skagit-river-bridge-colla-1785842162

Chapter 5: Arlington Memorial Bridge

1. "Memorial Bridge." National Park Service. https://www.nps.gov/nr/travel/wash/dc69.htm
2. Mike Murillo, "DC mayor makes plea for funds to fix Arlington Memorial Bridge." WTOP. January 7, 2017. http://wtop.com/local/2017/01/dc-mayor-makes-plea-funds-fix-arlington-memorial-bridge/
3. Nick Iannelli, "Plan set for badly needed Arlington Memorial Bridge repairs." WTOP. February 8, 2017. http://wtop.com/dc-transit/2017/02/arlington-memorial-bridge-repair-plan-picked/slide/1/

Chapter 6: Storrow Drive Overpass

1. Sarah L. Stewart, "America's most dangerous bridges." *Travel + Leisure*. August 5, 2013. http://www.travelandleisure.com/slideshows/americas-most-dangerous-bridges#no-1-storrow-drive-wb-over-storrow-drive-eb-storrow-drive-tunnel-boston
2. Shaun Ganley, "Boston home to worst bridge in America, survey finds." WCVB. August 5, 2017. http://www.wcvb.com/article/boston-home-to-worst-bridge-in-america-survey-finds/8186174
3. "Storrow Drive Tunnel named worst US bridge." Metro Boston. http://www.metro.us/local/boston-s-storrow-drive-tunnel-named-worst-bridge-in-america/tmWmhf---3fzEn2jpusd5E
4. "Is the Storrow Drive Overpass really the most dangerous bridge in America?" WGBH News. August 7, 2013. http://news.wgbh.org/post/storrow-drive-overpass-really-most-dangerous-bridge-america
5. Ibid.
6. David Boeri, "The Parkway known as Storrow Drive." WBUR. July 17, 2009. http://legacy.wbur.org/2009/07/17/esplanade-future
7. Ibid.

Chapter 7: Centennial Bridge

1. Jonathan Turner, "Iowa leads nation in 'structurally deficient' bridges." *Dispatch-Argus*. February 16, 2017. http://www.qconline.com/news/local/iowa-leads-nation-in-structurally-deficient-bridges/article_519f8d16-6fa4-5136-995a-3fab21191229.html
2. "Centennial Bridge." Johnweeks.com. https://www.johnweeks.com/river_mississippi/pagesB/umissB07.html
3. Turner, "Iowa leads nation."
4. Ibid.
5. Rock Island Centennial Bridge. Report. http://publications.iowa.gov/17670/1/IADOT_Rock_Island_Centennial_Bridge_1945.pdf
6. "Centennial Bridge." Johnweeks.com
7. Ibid.

Chapter 8: Greensboro Bridge

1. Mitch Carr, "Greensboro has the worst bridge in the state, according to AAA." Fox 8. May 31, 2013. http://myfox8.com/2013/05/24/substandard-bridges-in-the-piedmont/
2. Sarah Newell Williamson, "Worst Bridge in N.C.? It's in Guilford County." *Greensboro News & Record*, May 31, 2013. http://www.greensboro.com/news/local_news/worst-bridge-in-n-c-it-s-in-guilford-county/article_6c3d80d0-ca38-11e2-8dd2-001a4bcf6878.html
3. Taft Wireback, "AAA Carolinas: Greensboro bridge worst in state." *Greensboro News & Record*. July 18, 2014. http://www.greensboro.com/news/local_news/aaa-carolinas-greensboro-bridge-worst-in-state/article_dbfa4136-0e86-11e4-b843-001a4bcf6878.html

Charles River editors. *The Golden Gate Bridge: The History of San Francisco's Most Famous Bridge*. North Charleston, SC: CreateSpace Independent Publishing Platform, 2015.

Finger, Brad. *13 Bridges Children Should Know*. Munich, Germany: Prestel Junior, 2015.

Hurley, Michael. *The World's Most Amazing Bridges*. Mankato, MN: Raintree, 2011.

Latham, Donna. *Bridges and Tunnels: Investigate Feats of Engineering with 25 Projects*. White River Junction, VT: Nomad Press, 2012.

Stine, Megan. *Where Is the Brooklyn Bridge?* New York: Penguin, 2016.

ON THE INTERNET

Easy Science for Kids: Facts About Bridges for Kids
http://easyscienceforkids.com/all-about-bridges/

PBS. The Bridge Challenge
http://www.pbs.org/wgbh/buildingbig/bridge/challenge/index.html

Kidskonnect: Bridge Facts
https://kidskonnect.com/science/bridges/

WORKS CONSULTED

Adler, Jerry. "The history of the Verrazano-Narrows Bridge, 50 years after its construction." *Smithsonian*. November 2014. http://www.smithsonianmag.com/history/history-verrazano-narrows-bridge-50-years-after-its-construction-180953032/

Barone, Vincent. "Decades of construction being planned for Verrazano-Narrows Bridge." SILive.com. October 15, 2015. http://www.silive.com/news/2015/10/decades_of_necessary_construct.html

Boeri, David. "The Parkway known as Storrow Drive." WBUR. July 17, 2009. http://legacy.wbur.org/2009/07/17/esplanade-future

"Bridge-name gridlock: New York inches toward spelling error fix." *U.S. News*. June 23, 2017. https://www.usnews.com/news/best-states/new-york/articles/2017-06-23/bridge-name-gridlock-ny-inches-toward-spelling-error-fix

Burton, Lynsi. "The Skagit River bridge, 1 year after collapse." *Seattle Post-Intelligencer*. May 23, 2014. http://www.seattlepi.com/local/article/The-Skagit-River-bridge-1-year-after-collapse-5501507.php

Carr, Mitch. "Greensboro has the worst bridge in the state, according to AAA." Fox 8. May 31, 2013. http://myfox8.com/2013/05/24/substandard-bridges-in-the-piedmont/

"Centennial Bridge." Johnweeks.com. https://www.johnweeks.com/river_mississippi/pagesB/umissB07.html

"Did you know the Verrazano Bridge is spelled wrong?" *New York Post*. June 8, 2016. http://nypost.com/2016/06/08/did-you-know-the-verrazano-bridge-is-spelled-wrong/

"Frequently asked questions about the Golden Gate Bridge." Goldengatebridge.org. http://goldengatebridge.org/research/facts.php#SFChron

Ganley, Shaun. "Boston home to worst bridge in America, survey finds." WCVB. August 5, 2017. http://www.wcvb.com/article/boston-home-to-worst-bridge-in-america-survey-finds/8186174

Iannelli, Nick. "Plan set for badly needed Arlington Memorial Bridge repairs." WTOP. February 8, 2017. http://wtop.com/dc-transit/2017/02/arlington-memorial-bridge-repair-plan-picked/slide/1/

"Is the Storrow Drive Overpass really the most dangerous bridge in America?" WGBH News. August 7, 2013. http://news.wgbh.org/post/storrow-drive-overpass-really-most-dangerous-bridge-america

Jansen, Bart. "Study: 58,000 U.S. bridges found to be 'structurally deficient.'" *USA Today*. February 18, 2016. https://www.usatoday.com/story/news/2016/02/18/fewer-bridges-need-repairs-but-task-still-monumental/80512038/

Juliano, Frank. "Yankee Doodle Bridge work delayed until 2018." *Connecticut Post*. April 29, 2016. http://www.ctpost.com/local/article/Rehab-of-Yankee-Doodle-Bridge-over-I-95-pushed-7383820.php

Lindblom, Mike. "Skagit bridge documents: Did pilot-car pole strike crossbeams?" *Seattle Times*. June 11, 2014. http://blogs.seattletimes.com/today/2014/06/skagit-bridge-collapse-passing-trucker-thought-noise-was-a-bouncy-load/

"Memorial Bridge." National Park Service. https://www.nps.gov/nr/travel/wash/dc69.htm

Murillo, Mike. "DC mayor makes plea for funds to fix Arlington Memorial Bridge." WTOP. January 7, 2017. http://wtop.com/local/2017/01/dc-mayor-makes-plea-funds-fix-arlington-memorial-bridge/

Ouellette, Jennifer. "New analysis confirms why the Skagit River Bridge collapsed." Gizmodo. August 27, 2016. http://gizmodo.com/new-analysis-confirms-why-the-skagit-river-bridge-colla-1785842162

Radelat, Ana. "Report: Yankee Doodle Bridge in Norwalk 'structurally deficient.'" *Connecticut Mirror*. February 19, 2016. http://www.thehour.com/norwalk/article/Report-Yankee-Doodle-Bridge-in-Norwalk-8013016.php

Randall, Judy L. "A pothole-proof Verrazano? That's what engineers are promising." SILive. June 6, 2014. http://www.silive.com/news/index.ssf/2014/06/a_pothole-proof_verrazano_that.html

Schaub, Jeffrey. "The Golden Gate Bridge is starting to show its age." CBS Local. November 22, 2016. http://sanfrancisco.cbslocal.com/2016/11/22/the-golden-gate-bridge-is-starting-to-show-its-age/

Schmalz, Jeffrey. "Was Yankee Doodle fact or fiction? Debate rages on in Norwalk." *New York Times*. April 19, 1984. http://www.nytimes.com/1984/04/19/nyregion/was-yankee-doodle-fact-of-fiction-fight-rages-on-in-norwalk.html

"Silver Bridge." West Virginia Department of Transportation. http://www.transportation.wv.gov/highways/bridge_facts/Modern-Bridges/Pages/Silver.aspx

Standen, Amy. "75 years ago, a deadly day on the Golden Gate." NPR. May 27, 2012. http://www.npr.org/2012/05/27/153778083/75-years-later-building-the-golden-gate-bridge

Stewart, Sarah L. "America's most dangerous bridges." *Travel + Leisure*. August 5, 2013. http://www.travelandleisure.com/slideshows/americas-most-dangerous-bridges#no-1-storrow-drive-wb-over-storrow-drive-eb-storrow-drive-tunnel-boston

"Storrow Drive Tunnel named worst US bridge." Metro Boston. http://www.metro.us/local/boston-s-storrow-drive-tunnel-named-worst-bridge-in-america/tmWmhf---3fzEn2jpusd5E

Tiggiger, Annie. "Golden Gate Bridge facts and trivia." TripSavvy.com. August 3, 2016. https://www.tripsavvy.com/golden-gate-bridge-facts-and-trivia-2939802

"Travel + Leisure: Storrow Drive westbound bridge worst in U.S." MyFoxBoston.com. August 6, 2013. http://www.fox25boston.com/news/travel-leisure-storrow-drive-westbound-bridge-worst-in-us/140702851

Turner, Jonathan. "Iowa leads nation in 'structurally deficient' bridges." *Dispatch-Argus*. February 16, 2017. http://www.qconline.com/news/local/iowa-leads-nation-in-structurally-deficient-bridges/article_519f8d16-6fa4-5136-995a-3fab21191229.html

Williamson, Sarah Newell. "Worst Bridge in N.C.? It's in Guilford County." *Greensboro News & Record*, May 31, 2013. http://www.greensboro.com/news/local_news/worst-bridge-in-n-c-it-s-in-guilford-county/article_6c3d80d0-ca38-11e2-8dd2-001a4bcf6878.html

Wireback, Taft. "AAA Carolinas: Greensboro bridge worst in state." *Greensboro News & Record*. July 18, 2014. http://www.greensboro.com/news/local_news/aaa-carolinas-greensboro-bridge-worst-in-state/article_dbfa4136-0e86-11e4-b843-001a4bcf6878.html

GLOSSARY

architect (AHR-ki-tekt)—a person who designs buildings and other structures

boroughs (BUHR-ohs)—political divisions of New York City; they are The Bronx, Brooklyn, Manhattan, Queens, and Staten Island

corrosion (kuh-ROH-zhuhn)—slowly breaking apart or rusting

earmark (EER-mark)—to put money aside to pay for a project

engineers (in-juh-NEERZ)—people with scientific training who design and build structures such as bridges

infrastructure (IN-fruh-struk-shur)—the foundation or underlying physical structures of a country that allows its people to live comfortable lives

inspection (in-SPEK-shuhn)—the act of looking at something closely to learn if it has any flaws or problems

median (MEE-dee-uhn)—a grassy or paved area separating traffic going in opposite directions

pedestrian (puh-DES-tree-uhn)—person walking in areas near moving vehicles

restoration (reh-stuh-RAY-shuhn)—working to return something to its original condition

standards (STAN-derds)—levels of quality

sufficiency (suh-FISH-uhn-see)—having or providing as much as needed

suspension bridge (suh-SPEN-shuhn BRIJ)—bridge supported by two or more heavy cables held up by towers

INDEX

Akashi Kaikyo Bridge 8
American Automobile Association
    (Triple-A) 37
Arlington House 25
Arlington Memorial Bridge 25, 26
Aspiration and Literature (statue) 25
Belt Parkway 9
Boston, Massachusetts 28, 29, 30, 31
Bowser, Muriel 26
Brooklyn 6, 7
Cape Fear (movie) 38
Cape Fear Basin 38
Centennial Bridge 32, 33-35
Charles River 30
Connecticut 16, 17, 18, 19
Davenport, Iowa 33
Dohrn Transfer 35
Esplanade Park 30
Federal Highway Administration 27, 29
Fitch, Elizabeth 17
Fitch, Thomas 17
French and Indian War 17
Galbraith, Robert 34, 35
Golden Gate Bridge 11-15
Golden Gate Strait 11
Great Depression, The 11
Greensboro Bridge 36, 37-39
Greenwich 19
Guilford County 37
Illinois Department of Transportation 33
Iowa 18, 33
LaFave, Jim 22
Lee, Robert E. 25
Lincoln Memorial 25
Manus Bridge 19
Mills, Mike 38
Mississippi River 33, 35
Morrow, Irving 12
Mt. Vernon, Washington 21
Music and Harvest (statue) 25
Narrows Bridge 4
Nash, Robert 8
National Park Service 26, 27
New York Harbor 7
New York City 7, 14
North Carolina 37
Norwalk River 17

O'Connell, Sean 21
Oddo, James 8
Ohio 4
Ohio River 4
Pacific Ocean 11
Pennsylvania 18
Perry, Amanda 38
Potomac River 25
Rhode Island 18
Rock Island, Illinois 33
Sacrifice (statue) 25
San Francisco Bay 11
San Francisco, California 11, 15
Saugatuck River Bridge 19
Scott, William 21
Seattle, Washington 21
Shuckburgh, Richard 17
Silver Bridge 4
Skagit River Bridge 21-23
South Buffalo Creek 36, 37, 38, 39
Stark, Tim 22
Staten Island 7, 8
Staten Island Expressway 9
Storrow Drive Overpass 29
Storrow, Helen 31
Storrow, James 31
Storrow Road Tunnel 29, 30
suspension bridge 7
Tacoma, Washington 4
Tokyo, Japan 8
Travel + Leisure magazine 29
Trump, Donald 30
United States 4, 11, 29
United States Navy 13
U.S. Coast Guard 23
U.S. Department of Transportation 17, 37
Valor (statue) 25
Vancouver, Canada 21
Verrazzano, Giovanni da 7, 8
Verrazano-Narrows Bridge 7-9, 14
Virginia 25
Washington, D.C. 25
Wegmeyer, John 33
West Virginia 4
Whidbey Island Naval Air Station 23
Yankee Doodle (song) 17
Yankee Doodle Bridge 17-19

About the Author

Marty Gitlin is an educational book author based in Cleveland, Ohio. He has published more than 120 books for young readers since 2006. He won more than awards in 11 years as a newspaper journalist. Included was a first place for general excellence from the Associated Press. That organization also selected him as one of the top four feature writers in Ohio.